BEST.
Knock-knock
JOKES.
EVER

JOKES for KIDS

CHANTELLE GRACE

BroadStreet
KIDS

BroadStreet Kids
Savage, Minnesota, USA

BroadStreet Kids is an imprint of
BroadStreet Publishing Group, LLC.
Broadstreetpublishing.com

Best Knock-Knock Jokes Ever

978-1-4245-6296-1
978-1-4245-6297-8 (eBook)

Typeset and designed by | garborgdesign.com
Compiled and edited by Michelle Winger | literallyprecise.com

Printed in China.

21   22   23   24   25   26   7   6   5   4   3   2   1

CONTENTS

ANIMAL ANTICS

Knock, knock.

Who's there?

Hoo.

Hoo who?

You talk like an owl.

Knock, knock.

Who's there?

Goat.

Goat who?

Goat on a limb and open the door.

Knock, knock.

Who's there?

Lion.

Lion who?

Lion on your doorstep. Open up.

Knock, knock.

Who's there?

Dragon.

Dragon who?

Dragon your feet again?

Knock, knock.

Who's there?

Duck.

Duck who?

Just duck. They're throwing things at us.

6

Knock, knock.

Who's there?

Roach.

Roach who?

*Roach you an email last week
and haven't heard back.*

Knock, knock.

Who's there?

Kanga.

Kanga who?

No, it's kangaroo.

Knock, knock.

Who's there?

Toucan.

Toucan who

Toucan play that game.

Knock, knock.

Who's there?

Alpaca.

Alpaca who?

Alpaca the suitcase; you load the car.

Knock, knock.

Who's there?

Wood ant.

Wood ant who?

Wood ant harm a fly; don't worry.

Knock, knock.

Who's there?

Owl.

Owl who?

Owl good things come to those who wait.

Knock, knock.

Who's there?

Fleas.

Fleas who?

Fleas a jolly good fellow.

Knock, knock.

Who's there?

Honeybee.

Honeybee who?

Honeybee a doll and open the door.

Knock, knock.

Who's there?

Rhino.

Rhino who?

Rhino every knock-knock joke there is.

Knock, knock.

Who's there?

Rabbit.

Rabbit who?

Rabbit up carefully; it's fragile.

Knock, knock.

Who's there?

Herd.

Herd who?

Herd you were home, so can you come out?

Knock, knock.

Who's there?

Bee.

Bee who?

Bee at my house at hive-o-clock.

Knock, knock.

Who's there?

Gorilla.

Gorilla who?

Gorilla me a hamburger, please.

Knock, knock.

Who's there?

Whale.

Whale who?

Whale, whale, whale, what do we have here?

Knock, knock.

Who's there?

Chimp.

Chimp who?

Chimp off the old block.

Knock, knock.

Who's there?

Herring.

Herring who?

Herring some awful knock-knock jokes.

Knock, knock.

Who's there?

Sore ewe.

Sore ewe who?

*Sore ewe going to open the door
or not?*

Knock, knock.

Who's there?

Iguana.

Iguana who?

Iguana hold your hand.

Knock, knock.

Who's there?

Geese.

Geese who?

Geese what I'm going to do if you don't open the door?

Knock, knock.

Who's there?

Alligator.

Alligator who?

Alligator for her birthday was a card.

Knock, knock.

Who's there?

Bat.

Bat who?

Bat you'll never guess.

Knock, knock.

Who's there?

Howl.

Howl who?

Howl you know unless you open the door?

Why did the chicken cross the road?

To get to your house.

Knock, knock.

Who's there?

The chicken.

Knock, knock.

Who's there?

Cows go.

Cows go who?

No, cows go moo.

Knock, knock.

Who's there?

Bison.

Bison who?

Bison girl scout cookies, please.

Knock, knock.

Who's there.

Fangs.

Fangs who?

Fangs for letting me in.

19

Knock, knock.

Who's there?

Ruff.

Ruff who?

Ruff day. Let me in.

Knock, knock.

Who's there?

Owl.

Owl who?

Owl aboard.

Knock, knock.

Who's there?

Chimp.

Chimp who?

I think it's pronounced "shampoo."

Knock, knock.

Who's there?

Interrupting cow.

Interrupting cow wh...

Moo.

21

Knock, knock.

Who's there?

Laughing tentacles.

Laughing tentacles who?

You would laugh too if you had ten tickles.

Knock, knock.

Who's there?

Viper.

Viper who?

Viper nose; it's running.

22

NAME GAME

Knock, knock.

Who's there?

Luke.

Luke who?

Luke through the peephole and find out.

Knock, knock.

Who's there?

Duncan.

Duncan who?

Duncan my cookies in milk.
Can you open the door?

Knock, knock.

Who's there?

Goliath.

Goliath who?

Goliath down. You looketh tired.

Knock, knock.

Who's there?

Oswald.

Oswald who?

Oswald my bubblegum.

Knock, knock.

Who's there?

Teddy.

Teddy who?

Teddy is the beginning of the rest of your life.

Knock, knock.

Who's there?

Odysseus.

Odysseus who?

Odysseus the last straw.

Knock, knock.

Who's there?

Wendy.

Wendy who?

Wendy wind blows, it messes up my hair.

Knock, knock.

Who's there?

Ronde.

Ronde who?

Ronde vous here?

Knock, knock.

Who's there?

Barbara.

Barbara who?

Barbara black sheep, have you any wool?

Knock, knock.

Who's there?

Theresa.

Theresa who?

Theresa joke for everyone.

Knock, knock.

Who's there?

Rita.

Rita who?

Rita book of knock-knock jokes.

Knock, knock.

Who's there?

Alex.

Alex who?

Alex the questions around here.

Knock, knock.

Who's there?

Abbey.

Abbey who?

Abbey stung me on the arm.

Knock, knock.

Who's there?

Mikey.

Mikey who?

Mikey doesn't fit in the lock.

Knock, knock.

Who's there?

Rhoda.

Rhoda who?

Rhoda long way to get here;
now open up.

30

Knock, knock.

Who's there?

Avery.

Avery who?

Avery time I come to your house,
we go through this.

Knock, knock.

Who's there?

Mary.

Mary who?

Mary me?

31

Knock, knock.

Who's there?

Imena.

Imena who?

Imena pickle; open the door.

Knock, knock.

Who's there?

Noah.

Noah who?

Noah good place to eat?

Knock, knock.

Who's there?

Candice.

Candice who?

Candice door open or not?

Knock, knock.

Who's there?

Isma.

Isma who?

Isma lunch ready yet?

Knock, knock.

Who's there?

Alexia.

Alexia who?

Alexia again to open this door.

Knock, knock.

Who's there?

Toby.

Toby who?

Toby or not Toby, that is the question.

Knock, knock.

Who's there?

Abby.

Abby who?

Abby birthday to you.

Knock, knock.

Who's there?

Euripides.

Euripides who?

Euripides jeans; you pay for them.

35

Knock, knock.

Who's there?

Adolph.

Adolph who?

Adolph ball hit me in the mouth.

Knock, knock.

Who's there?

Aida.

Aida who?

Aida lot of sweets, and now I've got a tummy ache.

Knock, knock.

Who's there?

Horton hears a.

Horton hears a who?

I didn't know you liked Dr. Seuss.

Knock, knock.

Who's there?

Linda.

Linda who?

Linda hand, will you? Mine's tired from knocking.

Knock, knock.

Who's there?

Al.

Al who?

Al give you a hug if you open this door.

Knock, knock.

Who's there?

Aldo.

Aldo who?

Aldo anywhere with you.

Knock, knock.

Who's there?

Aladdin.

Aladdin who?

Aladdin the street wants a word with you.

Knock, knock.

Who's there?

Alec.

Alec who?

Alectricity. Isn't that a shock?

Knock, knock.

Who's there?

Anna.

Anna who?

Anna going to tell you.

Knock, knock.

Who's there?

Justin.

Justin who?

Justin time for dinner.

Knock, knock.

Who's there?

Doris.

Doris who?

Doris locked; that's why I knocked.

Knock, knock.

Who's there?

Aaron.

Aaron who?

Aaron you going to open the door?

Knock, knock.

Who's there?

Anita.

Anita who?

Anita borrow a key.

Knock, knock.

Who's there?

Alice.

Alice who?

Alice fair in love and war.

Knock, knock.

Who's there?

Nobel.

Nobel who?

Nobel. That's why I knocked.

Knock, knock.

Who's there?

Annie.

Annie who?

Annie thing you can do,
I can do better.

43

Knock, knock.

Who's there?

Theodore.

Theodore who?

Theodore is stuck, and it won't open.

Knock, knock.

Who's there?

Cher.

Cher who?

Cher would be nice if you opened the door.

Knock, knock

Who's there?

Amos.

Amos who?

Amos quito just bit me; hurry up.

Knock, knock.

Who's there?

Claire.

Claire who?

Claire a path; I'm coming through.

Knock, knock.

Who's there?

Norma Lee.

Norma Lee who?

Norma Lee I don't knock, but I am today.

Knock, knock.

Who's there?

Watson.

Watson who?

Watson TV? I'm coming in.

Knock, knock.

Who's there?

Iva.

Iva who?

*Iva sore hand from knocking.
Let me in.*

Knock, knock.

Who's there?

Sadie.

Sadie who?

Sadie magic word, and I'll come in.

47

Knock, knock.

Who's there?

Woo.

Woo who?

Oh, I'm so glad you're excited to see me.

Knock, knock.

Who's there?

Amanda.

Amanda who?

Amanda fix the lock on your door.

FOOD FRENZY

Knock, knock.

Who's there?

Cracker.

Cracker who?

*Cracker 'nother bad joke,
and I'm leaving.*

Knock, knock.

Who's there?

Butter.

Butter who?

Butter if you don't know.

Knock, knock?

Who's there?

Turnip.

Turnip who?

Turnip the volume; it's my favorite song.

50

Knock, knock.

Who's there?

Honeydew.

Honeydew who?

Honeydew you want to dance?

Knock, knock.

Who's there?

Lettuce.

Lettuce who?

Lettuce in, and you'll find out.

Knock, knock.

Who's there?

Ice cream.

Ice cream who?

Ice cream if you don't let me in.

Knock, knock.

Who's there?

Pecan.

Pecan who?

Pecan someone your own size.

Knock, knock.

Who's there?

Water.

Water who?

Water way to answer the door.

Knock, knock.

Who's there?

Figs.

Figs who?

Figs the doorbell; it's broken.

Knock, knock.

Who's there?

Cereal.

Cereal who?

Cereal pleasure to meet you.

Knock, knock.

Who's there?

Pudding.

Pudding who?

Pudding this package right here for you.

Knock, knock.

Who's there?

Ketchup.

Ketchup who?

Ketchup to me, and I will tell you.

Knock, knock.

Who's there?

Orange.

Orange who?

*Orange you going to answer
the door?*

Knock, knock.

Who's there?

Muffin.

Muffin who?

Muffin the matter with me; how about you?

Knock, knock.

Who's there?

Beets.

Beets who?

Beets me.

Knock, knock.

Who's there?

Olive.

Olive who?

Olive you.

Knock, knock.

Who's there?

Omelet.

Omelet who?

Omelet smarter than I look.

Knock, knock.

Who's there?

Doughnut.

Doughnut who?

Doughnut disturb me.

Knock, knock.

Who's there?

Carrot.

Carrot who?

Carrot all who this is?

Knock, knock.

Who's there?

Celery.

Celery who?

Celery isn't high enough. I quit.

Knock, knock.

Who's there?

Sultan.

Sultan who?

Sultan pepper.

Knock, knock.

Who's there?

Two fours.

Two fours who?

Two fours the door open would be bad.

Knock, knock.

Who's there?

Candy.

Candy who?

Candy cow jump over de moon?

Knock, knock.

Who's there?

Pasta.

Pasta who?

Pasta key, so I can open the door.

Knock, knock.

Who's there?

Thermos.

Thermos who?

Thermos be a better way to get a hold of you.

61

Knock, knock.

Who's there?

Cash.

Cash who?

No thanks, but I'd like some peanuts.

Knock, knock.

Who's there?

Broccoli.

Broccoli who?

Broccoli doesn't have a last name, silly.

Knock, knock.

Who's there?

Eggs.

Eggs who?

Eggscited to meet you.

Knock, knock.

Who's there?

Dishes.

Dishes who?

Dishes the last time I'll knock on your door.

63

FAMILY MATTERS

Knock, knock.

Who's there?

Nana.

Nana who?

Nana your business.

Knock, knock.

Who's there?

Honey.

Honey who?

Honey, I'm home.

Knock, knock.

Who's there?

Dishes.

Dishes who?

Dishes your mother. Open up.

Knock, knock.

Who's there?

Closure.

Closure who?

Closure mouth while you're eating, please.

Knock, knock.

Who's there?

Well not your parents

because they don't knock.

Knock, knock.

Who's there?

I'm T.

I'm T who?

Oh, you're only two? Is your mom home?

Knock, knock.

Who's there?

Cook.

Cook who?

Hey, I'm not crazy.

Knock, knock.

Who's there?

Cousin.

Cousin who?

Cousin my house, we open the door for family.

FUNNY PLACES

Knock, knock.

Who's there?

Hawaii.

Hawaii who?

Hawaii you? I'm fine.

Knock, knock.

Who's there?

Yukon.

Yukon who?

Yukon say that again.

Knock, knock.

Who's there?

Sweden.

Sweden who?

Sweden the coffee and open the door.

Knock, knock.

Who's there?

Amarillo.

Amarillo who?

Amarillo nice guy.

Knock, knock.

Who's there?

Irish.

Irish who?

Irish you would open the door.

71

Knock, knock.

Who's there?

Amish.

Amish who?

Really? You don't look like a shoe.

Knock, knock.

Who's there?

Safari.

Safari who?

Safari so good.

Knock, knock.

Who's there?

Adair.

Adair who?

Adair you to answer and find out.

Knock, knock.

Who's there?

Abyssinia.

Abyssinia who?

Abyssinia around lately.

73

Knock, knock.

Who's there?

Africa.

Africa who?

African love you.

Knock, knock.

Who's there?

Alaska.

Alaska who?

Alaska to open the door, please.

Knock, knock.

Who's there?

Iran.

Iran who?

Iran all the way here; I'm tired.

Knock, knock.

Who's there?

Europe.

Europe who?

No I'm not.

Knock, knock.

Who's there?

Armegeddon.

Armegeddon who?

Armegeddon a little bored.
Can you hurry up?

CRYPTIC MUCH?

Knock, knock.

Who's there?

You know.

You know who?

Exactly.

Knock, knock.

Who's there?

Adore.

Adore who?

Adore stands between us. Open up.

Knock, knock.

Who's there?

Me.

Me who?

You don't know who you are?

Knock, knock.

Who's there?

Police.

Police who?

Police let us in; it's cold out here.

Knock, knock.

Who's there?

See.

See who?

See you if you'll let me in.

Will you remember me in a month?

Yes.

Will you remember me in a week?

Yes.

Will you remember me in a day?

Yes.

Knock, knock.

Who's there?

See. You forgot me already.

Knock, knock.

Who's there?

Spell.

Spell who?

W-H-O.

Knock, knock.

Who's there?

Tank.

Tank who?

You're welcome.

Knock, knock.

Who's there?

Ya.

Ya who?

Actually, I prefer Google.

Knock, knock.

Who's there?

Cargo.

Cargo who?

Nope. Cargo beep.

Knock, knock.

Who's there?

Thumping.

Thumping who?

Thumping green and slimy is climbing up your back.

Knock, knock.

Who's there?

Boo.

Boo who?

Well, you don't have to cry about it.

83

Knock, knock.

Who's there?

Little old lady.

Little old lady who?

Wow. I didn't know you could yodel.

Knock, knock.

Who's there?

You.

You who?

You who! Let me in.

Knock, knock.

Who's there?

Stopwatch.

Stopwatch who?

Stopwatch you're doing and open the door.

Knock, knock.

Who's there?

I O.

I O who?

Me. When are you paying me back?

Knock, knock.

Who's there?

Control freak.

Control freak wh–

Okay, now you can say, "Control freak, who?"

Knock, knock.

Who's there?

A broken pencil.

A broken pencil who?

Never mind. It's pointless.

Knock, knock.

Who's there?

Avenue.

Avenue who?

Avenue opened this door before?

Knock, knock.

Who's there?

Says.

Says who?

Says me.

Knock, knock.

Who's there?

CD.

CD who?

CD person on your doorstep?
That's me.

Knock, knock.

Who's there?

No one.

No one who?

...

IT'S NATURAL

Knock, knock.

Who's there?

Heart.

Heart who?

Heart to hear you. Can you speak up?

Knock, knock.

Who's there?

Water.

Water who?

Water these plants, or they're going to die.

Knock, knock.

Who's there?

Leaf.

Leaf who?

Leaf me alone.

Knock, knock.

Who's there?

Snow.

Snow who?

Snow use. I forgot my name again.

Knock, knock.

Who's there?

Wire.

Wire who?

Wire you asking? I just told you.

Knock, knock.

Who's there?

Cotton.

Cotton who?

Cotton a trap; can you help me out?

Knock, knock.

Who's there?

Ash.

Ash who?

Bless you. I did not mean to make you sneeze.

Knock, knock.

Who's there?

Wooden shoe.

Wooden shoe who?

Wooden shoe like to know?

Knock, knock.

Who's there?

Mustache.

Mustache who?

Mustache you a question, but I'll shave it for later.

Knock, knock.

Who's there?

Radio.

Radio who?

Radio not; here I come.

Knock, knock.

Who's there?

Comb.

Comb who?

Comb on down and I'll tell you.

Knock, knock.

Who's there?

Icy.

Icy who?

Icy you looking at me.

Knock, knock.

Who's there?

Hike.

Hike who?

I didn't know you liked Japanese poetry.

Knock, knock.

Who's there?

Tree.

Tree who?

Treemendous to see you again.